MONUMENTAL REPUTATION
Robert Adam
&
the Emperor's Palace

RVINS OF THE PALACE
OF THE EMPEROR DIOCLETIAN
AT SPALATRO IN DALMATIA
BY R· ADAM F·R·S F·S·A
ARCHITECT TO THE KING
AND TO THE QVEEN
PRINTED FOR THE AVTHOR
MDCCLXIIII

Fig. 1. Robert Adam, 1728-1792. The architect holds a copy of what is thought to be his Ruins of the Palace of the Emperor Diocletian at Spalatro in Dalmatia. *The portrait is now attributed to David Martin.*

MONUMENTAL REPUTATION
Robert Adam
&
the Emperor's Palace

by
Iain Gordon Brown

NATIONAL LIBRARY OF SCOTLAND
EDINBURGH
1992

Published with the aid of a generous donation from
THE EDINBURGH ANTIQUES AND FINE ARTS SOCIETY

National Library of Scotland photographs by
S.W. McAvoy

Designed by
Derek Munn, HMSO Graphic Design, Edinburgh

*The illustration on the half-title is taken from Adam's title-page,
designed by Thomas Hollis to resemble a Roman inscription.*

ISBN 1 872116 02 7

PREFACE

In the course of assembling the materials for his great folio on the ruins of Diocletian's Palace at Split, Robert Adam was much concerned that he had not sufficient material, particularly engraved plates, to fill the volume which had been advertised.

No such qualms beset the author of a modest essay on the background to Adam's book, and the remarkable story of its making. The present brief work accompanies an exhibition, mounted to commemorate the bicentenary of Adam's death, which brings together a large number of drawings, engravings, books and manuscripts from many different collections. It makes no claim to be anything other than an exhibition companion: its structure is very closely related to that of the exhibition itself, echoing its themes and shape. I hope, nevertheless, that it may be of some lasting value as a succinct interpretation of a critical decade in Adam's life.

The idea for the exhibition arose from the suggestion by Professor Alistair Rowan that the National Library of Scotland should develop a major bicentenary display around the remarkable set of proof plates of the *Ruins at Spalatro* which had recently been purchased. This important document – consisting of proofs, some annotated in London by Robert Adam and his draughtsmen, and some in Venice by James Adam, who also recorded the observations of Charles-Louis Clérisseau, Robert's chief associate in the Diocletian's Palace project – is a source of unique significance for our understanding of the creation of a celebrated book. The set had been retained by Robert Adam as an 'office record' of how the book had taken shape. This acquisition has allowed the National Library to make a contribution to Adam scholarship rather beyond what it might be expected a library could do. Yet this is appropriate. Robert Adam was a leading figure of the Scottish Enlightenment, and the collection and preservation of the source materials for the study of all aspects of that social and cultural phenomenon – art and architectural history having their interests covered with all the rest – has long been a principal concern of the Departments of Manuscripts and Printed Books of the National Library. Nor should it be forgotten that Robert Adam was himself a bookman, that he had designed many celebrated country-house libraries, and that, towards the very end of his life, had proposed a superb building in Edinburgh to contain the Library of the Faculty of Advocates, that institution from which developed the National Library of today.

3 March 1992   I.G.B.

Robert Adam, an artist of genius arguably the greatest ever produced by Scotland, and one of the most outstanding talents in the history of British architecture, died in March 1792.

Today, the name of Adam is synonymous with the very idea of good taste and perfection of design. It conjures up, as does that of no other artist, the suggestion of gracious living; and it evokes, in a uniquely potent way, the elegant world of the British country house, and the urban refinement of an Edinburgh or London square.

Born in Kirkcaldy, educated in Edinburgh, trained in the family building and architectural practice, Robert Adam seized every opportunity to advance his career beyond what he saw as the narrow bounds of Scotland. On the Grand Tour he encountered Antiquity at the fountainhead in Rome, and, having acquired cosmopolitan learning and European sophistication, returned to establish himself in London.

An urbane gentleman of exquisite taste and profound antiquarian erudition, he rapidly became the darling of the salon and the drawing-room, and early reached the summit of his profession as the most fashionable architect of the day.

By the brilliance of his vision, and through his tireless energy, he formed an eclectic and distinctive style of architecture and interior decoration, in which the great inspiration of classical antiquity, abstracted, revised, reconstituted and rendered back, was blended with elements of many other periods. Adam's hallmark as an interior architect was the application of an infinite repertoire of decorative detail in apartments distinguished by the intricate planning of interconnecting rooms in a variety of shapes. This manner was soon identified with Adam's name. Few architects, indeed, have merited the supreme accolade of an eponymous style.

In the practice of his art, Adam claimed to 'seize the beautiful spirit of antiquity and to transfuse it, with novelty and variety, through all our numerous works'. To have brought about 'a kind of revolution' was his proudest boast.

In 1764, Robert Adam published a magnificent book: *Ruins of the Palace of the Emperor Diocletian at Spalatro in Dalmatia.*

Adam's book was the outcome of an expedition to Split – then called Spalato (or, by Adam, Spalatro) – in the Venetian territories of the eastern Adriatic coast, now part of present-day Croatia. His journey to Spalato, and his survey of the Roman ruins there, had been the culmination of his Grand Tour of 1754-58.

The theme of this essay, and the exhibition which it accompanies, is the making of Adam's book in the context of his European education, and in that of his driving ambition to the leading architect of his age. The subject is examined in the light of his archaeological interests as these developed in Italy, and his growing familiarity with the full range of Roman architectural and decorative forms. The aim is to trace the complex and convoluted history of the creation of a beautiful book which is one of the masterpieces of eighteenth-century printing and engraving. It will be seen how self-improvement was followed by self-advertisement, and how these led to self-fulfilment in Adam's spectacular success. At its broadest, the subject is that ten-year period which saw Adam's career transformed, and which set him

on the road to the achievement of his Monumental Reputation.

Fig. 2. Matthias Darly: 'The Antique Architect', a caricature of Robert Adam, 1773.

When Robert Adam left Scotland for Italy and the adventure which would change his life, he had already acquired considerable experience in his profession. For he was the son of Scotland's leading architect, contractor, and builders' merchant; and all of William Adam's sons – of whom Robert was the second – followed their father in his callings.

John Clerk of Eldin (Robert Adam's exact contemporary, the son of one of William Adam's most important patrons, and later to be Robert's brother-in-law), gave this appealing assessment of the young Adam in an unpublished memoir: 'Besides the closest application to drawing and the other necessary studies in his profession [he] was of such a lively genius & spirit that from his early youth, and

through the whole course of his life, he was the darling & the admiration of the numerous men of genius of the age which resorted to his father's house...'.

Robert rapidly emerged as the most brilliant and ambitious member of what was in effect a family firm. He had mastered the elements of all the branches of the building trades and the architectural profession: Government contracting for the Board of Ordnance at Fort George, near Inverness; assisting his elder brother John with the finishing of Inveraray Castle for the 3rd Duke of Argyll; completing, again with John, a modified version of their father's grandiose design for Hopetoun House, and creating (perhaps) the sumptuous decorative scheme for its state rooms; designing and beginning to build, with John, as their first major independent commission, Dumfries House for the 4th Earl of Dumfries. Robert had made connexions, and he had made money. At the age of twenty-five, he estimated his share of the family capital at £5,000. The money paid for his European travels; and his contacts with the Scottish aristocracy allowed him to move in elevated circles both at home and abroad.

In 1754 he considered that the time had come to make an investment in himself.

Fig. 3.   *Building operations of the mid-eighteenth century: decorative design by C.-N. Cochin, whom Robert Adam met in Paris.*

In the eighteenth century, the more an architect was shown to understand the buildings and decoration of the classical past, the more he was presumed to be capable of achieving in his own practice. The young architect studied Antiquity, and drew the remains of the past, so that he himself might design and build for the present, and thus for the future.

Robert Adam's Grand Tour was a remarkable adventure of archaeological and architectural discovery. We know more about his European education than we do about the travels, hopes and inspiration of any other British artist. Some hundreds of letters to his relations have come down to us to tell of the experiences and artistic development of 'Bob the Roman', as he called himself.

Fig. 4.   A young architect sketching ruins: decorative design drawn and engraved by P.-E. Babel, recommended to Adam when in Paris as 'a good man to do any ornaments for our books'.

The great catalyst of his life was the pursuit of Antiquity – 'the Antique, the Noble & the Stupendous' – in these Italian years, when he encountered at first hand the ancient sources, and discovered by archaeological investigation the infinite variety of Roman decorative detail and of Imperial domestic planning. Adam, who had considered himself well trained in draughtsmanship and construction, had to unlearn his book-learning, and begin his studies anew. His school became the ruins themselves.

Adam wanted to be noticed as an architect, and archaeology was to be a means to that end. *Spalatro* was a work of archaeological and architectural scholarship, designed to enhance his reputation and to advance his career. He had early appreciated the potential advantages of publishing a handsome book which would, as he said, 'introduce me into England with an uncommon splendour'. A lavish folio on some ancient site would be 'a great puff, conducive to raising all at once one's name & character'. There was a further, practical reason for producing an archaeological book at the outset of an architectural career. Such a publication might impress by a display of knowledge, taste and ability through the interpretation of the past. The author might gain reputation while avoiding premature criticism of his own architecture, and the risk of his designs being plagiarized: 'Your fame spreads in a more polite way, & every dirty artist in London has them not to spit at over a mug of porter'. As for connoisseurs, 'they could not miss to admire one who knew all the antiquities to an inch, nor would they be able to find any criticisms not having any of my own designs to object to'.

Fig. 5. An allegory of the sources of neo-classicism. The caption reads: 'A student conducted to Minerva, who points to Greece, and Italy, as the Countries from whence he must derive the most perfect Knowledge & Taste in elegant Architecture'. Engraving by Bartolozzi after a painting by A. P. Zucchi.

By the time that Robert Adam went abroad, the 'Grand Tour' had long been an established part of the education of the well-born or well-to-do young man. Most of these *milordi inglesi* or *cavalieri scozzesi* looked on the experience principally as an agreeable diversion during which they might acquire an additional polish, and such knowledge of classical art and architecture as it was expected a gentleman should have.

Robert Adam, by contrast, though he indulged fully in the hectic social life of the great cities of France and Italy, had a more serious purpose. For him, Florence and Rome were more than mere places of carnival entertainment, with some statues and buildings added as cultural seasoning. In a memor-

Fig. 6.   G. B. Piranesi: Grand Tourists admiring the stucco decorations in the tomb of the Arruntii, Rome.

able phrase, Rome was for Adam his 'Holy See of pleasurable Antiquity'.

'Rome is the most glorious place in the universal world. A grandeur & tranquillity reigns in it, everywhere noble & striking remains of antiquity appear in it, which are so many that one who has spent a dozen years in seeing is still surpris'd with something new. The hills it stands on give you everywhere elevated prospects of town and country – the town rich with domes, spires & lofty buildings, ancient & modern; the country near Rome uneven, hilly, woody & adorned with villas, villages & churches, so that had one their friends nothing could persuade one to quit it for any other part I ever saw. In fine, for a man of taste the day is too short, as you never tire of the agreeable, grand & picturesque walks... In short, I am antique mad, or what they would call in Scotland an Antick. But antique here, antique there, I hope to be able to invent great things if I shou'd never be able to execute one – & that's my ambition.'

He set himself to look and learn more intently than anyone had ever done. He formed friendships with leading artists, architects and archaeologists. He assembled a team of assistants and draughtsmen. He measured the monuments, and sketched among the ruins. He exercised his imagination in the design of fantasy architecture based on what he had seen in the ruins of the baths and villas of ancient Rome, and drew inspiration not only from the antiquities, but also from the fortifications and palaces of the Renaissance, from the Vatican *loggie* and the stucco grotesques of the Villa Madama, and even from the Baroque Rome of the Popes. He conceived the idea of making his name by writing a major work on Roman monuments; but in the end he elected to publish a study, not of a majestic building in the Eternal City itself, nor of a great Hadrianic site such as the imperial villa at Tivoli, with its daring experiments in vaulting, but rather of a late, provincial monument: the Palace at Spalato.

Fig. 7.   G. B. Piranesi: Piazza del Popolo, gateway to Rome from the north, with its Egyptian obelisk, the twin churches of Santa Maria dei Miracoli and Santa Maria di Monte Santo, and the three streets radiating out towards the heart of Rome.

In Italy Robert Adam lived a double life. His daily round combined, as he put it, 'the genteel with the studious'. 'Now these days [of Carnival] being over, I am again return'd to my studies – to feast on marble ladies, to dance attendance in the chamber of Venus, and to trip a minuet with old Otho, old Cicero, and those other Roman worthies whose very busts seem to grin contempt at my legerity. Now I spend the night among virtuosi and their works... Now and then I launch out into the fine world, and again I retire among my worthy connoisseurs and virtuosi. In one hour I doat upon my Marquis Corsi, next you see me among a heap of portfolios.'

On the one hand, he was a social gadabout, taking part in the round of assemblies, balls and *conversazioni*, the Carnivals of Florence and Rome, and the decadent voluptuousness of Venice; the worldly and pleasure-loving companion of Contessas and Cardinals in the princely *palazzi* of contemporary cities. To this elevated world he was a Scottish gentleman, of cultivated tastes and artistic inclinations certainly, but nothing resembling a mere professional who had already earned, and who intended to earn his future living through the practice of architecture. Adam had asked his family not to put 'Architect' on letters addressed to him. Even among fellow-students and lesser artists (as he saw them), to whom his interests were known, Adam played the great gentleman and patron: 'I am here like the King of Artists, & have flocks of them daily about me, who come to pay court to me. They are highly honour'd when I give them, their wives or daughters, a twirl in my coach which, provided they are handsome, I never fail to do'.

On the other hand, as the serious and industrious antiquary and student of architecture, he moved in a circle of distinguished *cognoscenti* – men of the calibre of Cardinal Alessandro Albani, Count Francesco Algarotti, Giovanni Battista Piranesi, and his fellow-countrymen Allan Ramsay and Robert Wood, who were eminent scholars at large in Rome. To these he was a complete professional, determined to win their respect as artist, scholar and connoisseur. With Piranesi and with Ramsay, for example, he went on sketching expeditions, exploring the baths and villas of ancient Rome and the Campagna, and he noted, especially, the stucco decorations – the *grotesques* – in subterranean tombs and vaults. This archaeological knowledge would be of particular importance in the evolution of his own decorative style.

Fig. 8. A trompe l'œil *sketch of a group of architectural* capricci *and drawings of Roman ruins by Robert Adam. He called such compositions 'sketches of taste and invention'.*

Fig. 9. G. B. Piranesi: *title-page of* Il Campo Marzio dell' Antica Roma, *illusionistically etched as if it were a time-worn Latin inscription, against which is propped an altar bearing the name of Robert Adam.*

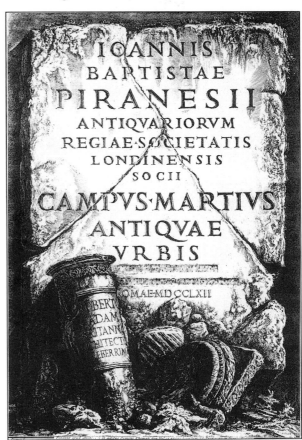

In Florence Adam had met the French architect and architectural draughtsman Charles-Louis Clérisseau. The Frenchman specialized in drawing romantic compositions of imaginary ruins, or groups of actual ruins and buildings rearranged in picturesque landscapes – *capricci* or fantasies – and Adam was taught by him to look at Antiquity and the remains of the past in a new way. 'I have found a gentleman ... who will put me on a method of improving myself more in drawing & architecture than I ever had any ideas of', Robert later wrote of Clérisseau: '...the utmost knowledge of architecture, of perspective, & of designing & colouring I ever saw or had any conception of. He raised my ideas. He created emulation & fire in my breast. I wished above all things to learn his manner, to have him with me at Rome, to study close with him....'.

Adam persuaded Clérisseau to accompany him to Rome, there to enjoy an ambivalent position partly as his artistic mentor, partly as his assistant: Clérisseau was both teacher and dependant. However cocksure Adam may have appeared, or however insufferable seemed his opinions in respect of his own abilities, and the lack of talent among the run of his contemporaries – he was to refer to them as 'Reptile Architects' – privately he was remarkably clear-eyed about his deficiencies. He realized that he had everything to learn. This he admitted only to his family back in Edinburgh. 'To be the man I may be,

Fig. 10.   *Pier Leone Ghezzi: caricature of Charles-Louis Clérisseau*

much is to be done & I don't exaggerate when I assure you I as yet, with all I have seen, studied & done hitherto, think myself a mere beginner.' His architectural education began again under Clérisseau's direction. In him Adam recognized that he had found 'a most valuable & ingenious creature', from whom he might learn to draw in what he called 'the Grand Style'.

In Rome Adam gathered to Clérisseau and himself, and to his French tutors in figure and landscape drawing, a number of young draughtsmen to whom he referred, like some latter-day hero of the Trojan War, as his 'Myrmidons of Art'. And like some artistic Achilles, Adam prepared to do battle in the future with any Hector who arose to challenge him, be he an older contemporary like William Chambers, or a younger man like Robert Mylne. Headquarters was established at Casa Guarnieri, which was at once fashionable residence, drawing-office, and gallery for the display of Adam's artistic taste and talent.

It was this team – comprising Adam as director and paymaster, yet student too; Clérisseau as artistic adviser; and the youths to record what the Scotsman and the Frenchman told them to do – which began to work on a number of grand antiquarian projects. The ultimate aim was glorification of the name of Adam through potential publications, and thus the enhancement of his standing as scholar and architect on his eventual return to Britain.

Fig. 11. Felice Polanzani: portrait of Giovanni Battista Piranesi, 'part modern man, part antique fragment'

With Clérisseau to stimulate his already rich imagination, and under the influence of Piranesi, whose vision of antiquity and the grandeur of Imperial Rome so inspired his own, Adam began to draw a series of ever more febrile and astonishing architectural fantasies.

The relationship with Piranesi was of enormous importance for Adam's archaeological and architectural awakening. Piranesi, as Adam wrote, might be said to 'breathe the ancient air': the young Scotsman learned much from the Venetian's 'amazing & ingenious fancies ... produced in the different plans of the Temples, Baths & Palaces ... the greatest fund

for inspiring and instilling invention in any lover of architecture that can be imagined'. The admiration was, apparently, mutual. Piranesi, wrote Adam, 'imagined at first that I was like the other English who had a love of antiques without knowledge'; but upon 'seeing some of my sketches & drawings was so highly delighted that he almost ran quite distracted & said I have more genius for the true noble architecture than any Englishman ever was in Italy'. The second benefit to Adam from the friendship came in the form of a 'public relations' coup. Adam was able to extract from Piranesi some remarkable tributes in the form of dedications, flattering allusions, and half-concealed references in etchings

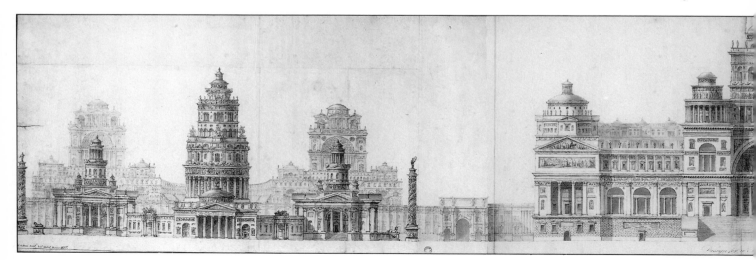

illustrating some of Piranesi's most spectacular, powerful and polemical works on Roman monuments.

Fig. 12.   *Robert Adam: architectural fantasy.*
A composition of a colonnade, a portico and a round tower built against an embankment, the buttresses of which may echo those of the substructures of the Palatine.

Fig. 13.   *Robert Adam: design for a palace, Rome 1757.*
Many antique and Renaissance sources are laid under tribute. The drawing is more than nine feet long.

In Adam's drawings of vast palatial complexes, the most recognizable source is that of the architecture of the Roman *thermae*, with their intricate and varied planning of interior space, their great, intersecting, vaulted halls, and extensive colonnades. Also much in evidence is the distinctive circular form of the Pantheon, greatest of all surviving Roman buildings, distinguished externally by its saucer dome; and triumphal columns, arches, and temple porticoes also appear.

In this predilection for conceiving palaces so vast as never to be capable of realization, Adam was not alone. Several young architects working in mid-eighteenth-century Rome drew similar designs. The theme was often a huge and spreading royal palace (such as James Adam was later to plan), or a towering monument to national glory. But some of Adam's designs are especially astounding, and incorporate elements from ancient Roman, Romanesque, medieval castellated, ecclesiastical Gothic, Renaissance and even Baroque architecture, all contributing to the megalomaniac dream – but a dream, nevertheless, of profound and original genius.

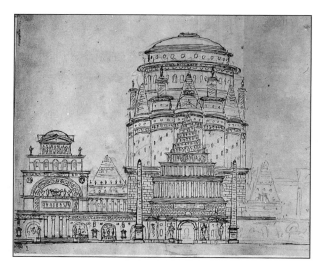

Fig. 14.   Robert Adam: architectural fantasy. This is one of Adam's most astonishing designs, though heavily influenced by Piranesi.

Fig. 15.   Robert Adam: design for a palace.

Adam's time in Rome coincided with a great age of archaeological book-publishing. He knew, either personally or by repute, many of the protagonists in this movement, an episode which is not purely a bibliographical phenomenon but a watershed in the history of taste. The monuments of Greece, the Aegean and the Levant had been surveyed to the most exacting standards; and forgotten desert cities were being published in opulent folio volumes which opened a new world to connoisseurs. All the talk was of expeditions, of subscription-lists, of books in the making, or rival projects.

Naturally Adam was not one to remain immune from this fever. He saw the possibility of establishing an architectural reputation through archaeological publishing. There were several patterns to follow, and forerunners to better. He might dream,

Fig. 16.   J.-D. Le Roy: archaeological exploration in the Aegean.

after a good dinner with the painter Gavin Hamilton, where the talk had been of Egypt, of 'arts & sciences, of Greece & the Grecian Islands', of finishing in three months 'a very tolerable work to

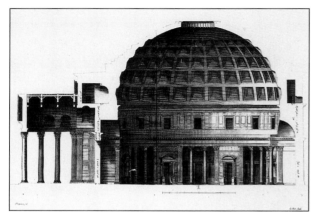

Fig. 17. *Antoine Desgodetz: longitudinal section of the Pantheon.*

rival Stuart & Rivet (sic)', and of then returning home 'laden with laurel'. Nevertheless, he had already Roman schemes a-plenty to pursue, being 'determin'd, in imitation of Scotch heroes, to become author, to attack Vitruvius, Palladio, & those blackguards of ancient & modern architecture, sword in hand'.

James Stuart and Nicholas Revett, in the work which would eventually lead to *The Antiquities of Athens*, and Robert Wood and his collaborators, in the explorations which would result in the *Ruins of Palmyra* and *Balbec*, took as their model of scrupu-

lously accurate recording of measurements the great survey of the monuments of Rome by Antoine Desgodetz (1682). Adam made his first publishing project in Rome the production of a revised edition of Desgodetz – long out of print, in French, and almost unobtainable. Towards this aim a great deal of work was done, and many drawings collected: Adam was damning of the 'bungling researches' of

Fig. 18.   *Robert Adam: vault in the Large Baths of Hadrian's Villa at Tivoli, showing stucco 'grotesques'.*

his contemporaries, and boasted that his new surveys of the *thermae* in particular would be 'a most glorious work to which your Palmyras and Balbecs are less than nothing & vanity'. 'I would not want the satisfaction of having the studies of these Baths & other things in Rome for any consideration, as, if ever Fortune shoud favour me highly, I may have the opportunity of reviving something of the Old Style in England.'

As it happened, the full Desgodetz revision proved too large an undertaking, and Adam turned to concentrate on specific buildings or complexes which had figured in the larger survey: to Hadrian's Villa at Tivoli, and especially to the Baths of Caracalla and Diocletian. The *thermae* project, arguably the most valuable of Adam's Roman surveys, comprehended a revision of the plans, sections and elevations made by Palladio and published as *Fabbriche Antiche* by Lord Burlington; and although Adam never produced the book he might have done on that subject – it was left to Charles Cameron to publish a revision and elaboration of Palladio's drawings – the planning and decoration of these great ruins influenced profoundly his emerging style, and his vision of 'the Grand'.

Fig. 19. *Andrea Palladio: sections through the baths of Diocletian. Robert Adam sought to improve upon these records, engraved by Paul Fourdrinier from drawings by Isaac Ware after Palladio's original drawings.*

Adam's desire to appear as the author of a major publication that would engage the attention of both the fashionable and learned worlds and which would help to establish his reputation, and his concurrent interest in the design of grandiose palaces of fantasy, coalesced in his eventual choice of archaeological project.

An actual palace, a monument of late Antiquity, but nevertheless a complex building of considerable splendour, was located conveniently close across the Adriatic Sea and easily reachable from Venice. Had time and money been no object, Adam would have chosen to extend his travels beyond Italy to Greece, or to Asia Minor and possibly as far as the Levant. But he feared that time spent in further study abroad would give his rivals, notably William Chambers (who had already completed his training in Paris and Rome, and was by then architectural tutor to the Prince of Wales – the future George III), too great a head start in the race for architectural commissions and celebrity at home in Britain.

Thus the Emperor Diocletian's Palace at Spalato, a site not well known and not the subject of any detailed topographical or architectural survey, suggested itself as the answer to Adam's need. He himself, in the unpublished draft preface to his book,

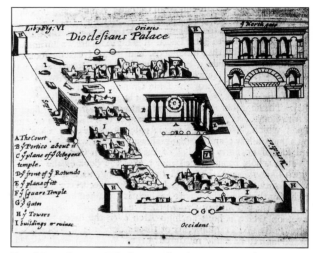

Fig. 20.   *George Wheler: crude plan (1682) of Diocletian's Palace, with elevation of the Porta Aurea.*

suggested that what he called the 'jaunt to Dalmatia' and the Spalato project arose directly from his earlier work on Diocletian's Baths in Rome. Here he expressed admiration for Diocletian as a great builder, praising 'the delicacy of his Taste'. 'These circumstances [Adam's work on the *thermae*], together with what I had both heard and read of a private Palace which that Emperor had built ... convinced me that I might there find somethng worthy of Publick attention... But what still further excited my Curiosity was the hopes of throwing some new lights upon the private Buildings of the Ancients, a subject which had hitherto been so superficially handled that I doubted not it would render such an undertaking still more acceptable to the publick.'

In the choice of Spalato was an element of convenience. Adam did not suggest that the Palace was the greatest building of the Ancient World, although it was certainly a rare example of a private rather than a public edifice. But it was the best thing he could find to suit his purposes in the circumstances. The selection of Spalato was an example of the opportunism inherent in Adam's character.

Fig. 21.   J. B. Fischer von Erlach: reconstruction (early eighteenth century) of Diocletian's Palace. The coin inset at top right was issued to mark the twentieth year (vicennalia) of the Emperor's reign.

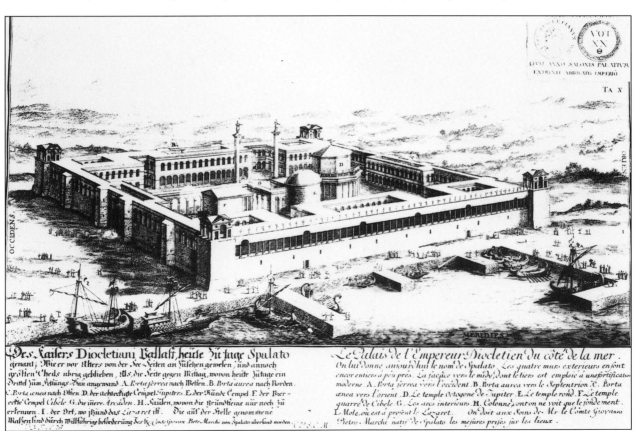

Diocletian, a native of Dalmatia and a man of low birth, came to the imperial purple through military power at a time of crisis in AD 284. His rule was marked by a genius for administration. He reorganized the civil, military and fiscal machinery of empire. The whole structure of imperial power was changed by the institution of the Tetrarchy, whereby Diocletian took a co-emperor to rule with him (one to be responsible for the East, one for the West) and each adopted a junior partner to assist him.

Diocletian's rule took on aspects of a theocracy: it was government by 'divine right', in almost Oriental majesty, with devotion to the old gods of Rome and severe persecution of the Christians. For administrative convenience, the provinces were divided into smaller units; but in time a vast administrative structure led to an overwhelming bureaucracy.

In 305 Diocletian abdicated, and retired to his homeland where, near the town of Salona, he built a palatial villa – a fortified residence combining elements in character military, urban and those of a private dwelling. It was really a villa for retirement

Fig. 22. Ernst Hébrard: reconstruction (early twentieth century) of Diocletian's Palace.

(however grand) and not a palace for a reigning emperor, with all the ceremonial features that would have dictated. Here Diocletian's concern was (as later historians observed) the cultivation of his cabbages.

Though others before him had made records of a kind, Adam was the first to make a systematic survey of the ruins. By 1757, what had begun as a retirement villa for a sometime emperor had for more than a thousand years been the centre of the flourishing port and town of Spalato, the buildings of which had filled up the area within the palace walls, overlying the Roman structures, and had extended beyond them. The site had the quality of a palimpsest.

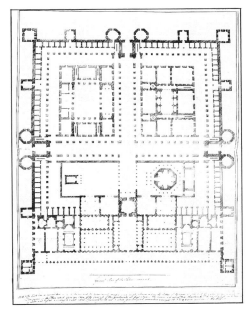

Fig. 23.   Robert Adam: annotated proof of plan of the Palace, restored.

Adam and his 'Myrmidons' spent only five weeks at Spalato, but his book was some seven years in the making.

Examination of the Adam family correspondence, and the evidence of the original drawings in St Petersburg, London, Cambridge and elsewhere, together with the information furnished by the annotated proofs in the National Library set of engraved plates, give an unparalleled insight into the way in which a great illustrated book was produced in the eighteenth century. It is a story of unique complexity; and indeed it is difficult to conceive of a more inconvenient way of making a book than appears to have been the case with *Spalatro*.

The picturesque views, perspectives, and romanticized topographical drawings of the principal buildings and townscape, were done by Clérisseau. Adam's team of draughtsmen presumably was responsible for the measured drawings which form the greater part of the book. Finished drawings would be worked up from sketches made on site. These original drawings – the views, and the elevations, sections and architectural details – then had to be engraved.

First, with reproduction in mind, a specially adapted drawing had to be prepared for the engraver. The

Figs. 24-25.   F. Bartolozzi after C.-L. Clérisseau: avant la lettre proof of the view of Spalato from the south west, and a detail. When engraving this view Bartolozzi put his name ('Fran. Bartolozzi/ Fiorentino/ 1759') on the fountain in the right foreground. In the second state plate this is crudely hatched out; but at least the engraver was ultimately given the credit for the plate.

painstaking and highly skilled work of engraving, which involved transfer of the graphic image, in reverse, to a copper plate, was undertaken partly in Venice, partly in London, by artists who were among the leading engravers of the day. We find that at this stage many of the original compositions were altered, particularly in the matter of the introduction of figure groups to give atmospheric effect to the finished engraving. Proofs of the engravings were sent back and forward so that they might be checked for accuracy against the original drawings, or the memory of either Adam or Clérisseau, the one in London, the other in Venice, each with only some of the complete set of drawings, the plates to be altered or retouched accordingly. The actual copperplates which had been engraved in Venice – and some were subsequently retouched in Rome – were finally trundled by wagon, at hazard from looters, across a Europe ravaged by the Seven Years War. In London the copperplates were lettered – titles and key letters being added – and there the introduction

to the book, and the commentary on the plates, were printed on paper bought in Rome.

Figs. 26-27.   F. Bartolozzi after C.-L. Clérisseau: plate from Spalatro, *and a detail of this, showing how Clérisseau and Bartolozzi made whimsical attempts to record their contribution to the book by putting their names on a sarcophagus: 'Hic iacet corpus Clerissi pictoris', etc. Adam failed to notice this not very serious bid for recognition.*

Although Robert Adam's name adorns the title-page, which is set out like a Roman inscription, *Spalatro* is in fact the work of many hands and minds.

When Adam conceived his first publishing project – the revision of Desgodetz – he had intended that Clérisseau should contribute perspective views of the monuments, work which the Frenchman would 'undertake for me with infinite satisfaction & [would] execute with thorough beauty and justice'. It was this aspect of the enterprise at Spalato which would be Clérisseau's responsibility. Yet Adam withheld from Clérisseau any credit for his work. In his manuscript preface, Adam referred to Clérisseau as an agreeable companion and inspiring guide in archaeological and architectural matters. He omitted to mention that Clérisseau had been expected to make an important material contribution to the success of the volume. After prolonged family debate, and much soul-searching, Adam stopped short at putting his own name to the plates as artist, but omitted any attribution to Clérisseau of the perspective views. Only the names of engravers are given. The implication, though not the explicit statement, was that all the plates were drawn by Robert Adam himself. Here Adam was taking the risk of exposure as a cheat. For he had learned from Consul Smith that Clérisseau had been showing around in Venice the drawings he had made at Spalato, and that he was known as the artist, thus effectively queering the pitch for Adam in his intent to claim them as his. Adam's reaction is amusing in its disingenuousness: '... really things of that nature are hurtful & vexatious, that after you carry one about with you, pay him handsomely & as a friend, that he should out of meer Vanity do so unfriendly an action...'.

Nor was Adam the author of the Introduction to the book. As family correspondence makes clear, Adam's cousin, the distinguished historian William Robertson, was persuaded to write the text, for which he was paid ten cases of claret. Furthermore, much of the management of the book's production was handled by James Adam, Robert's younger brother, who had followed him to Italy on his own Grand Tour. James played a major role in the supervision of the engraving of the plates, spending a great deal of time in Venice (and later in Rome) keeping Robert's temperamental Italian draughtsmen and engravers up to the mark, and in the general co-ordination of the whole enterprise.

THE *SPALATRO* DRAMATIS PERSONAE

Author & Project Director
ROBERT ADAM

Project Manager
James Adam

Copywriter & Historical Adviser
William Robertson

Principal Artist & Perspective Draughtsman
Charles-Louis Clérisseau

Draughtsmen
Agostino Brunias
Laurent-Benôit Dewez

Adviser at Spalato
Count Antonio Marković

Agent in Venice
Consul Joseph Smith

Venetian Engraving Team
Francesco Bartolozzi, Francesco Zucchi,
Paolo Santini
& other gentlemen

Roman Engraving Team
Domenico Cunego & other gentlemen

London Engraving Team
Edward Rooker, Francis Patton, Anthony Walker,
James Basire, Peter Mazell, John Green,
& other gentlemen

London Figure Draughtsman
Paul Sandby

Reader & Referee
Johann Joachim Winckelmann

Title-page Designer
Thomas Hollis

Printer
William Strahan

Supporters & Confidantes
('A Council & Quorum of wise and considerate
Friends')
Mary Adam (née Robertson), mother
Janet (Jenny), Margaret (Peggy), Helen (Nelly),
Elizabeth (Betty) Adam, sisters.

Robert Adam himself, in writing of the problems of, first, the archaeological investigation of an ancient structure, and, secondly, the subsequent architectural restoration of the

Fig. 28.   Frontispiece of Adam's book, a capriccio *which includes elements of some four of the monuments at Spalato, with one from elsewhere. The quasi-Roman inscription is a roughly equivalent Latin translation of the English title of the book.*

building in the form of geometrical elevations and plans on paper, stressed the inherent dichotomy between the realms of 'truth' and 'fancy'. As far as these abstractions influenced Adam in the production of *Spalatro*, Truth represented the evidence of archaeological investigation and architectural record – what his contemporaries Wood, Stuart and Revett called Accuracy; and Fancy represented that element of personal interpretation which at its most extreme led to imaginative reconstruction rather beyond the limits of the evidence. Fancy, which furthermore implied the intervention of judgment, was also equated by Adam with Taste.

The mid-eighteenth-century author of an archaeological book – or, more accurately, a work that combined archaeology, architecture and topographical record, with a taste of exotic travel – would be expected to produce something of a compromise: a volume embracing elements of the technical treatise with measured drawings and scholarly text, and the pictorial folio emphasizing the romance of antiquity. In a book of this type, measured drawings of cornice mouldings, column bases and ceiling coffers were interspersed with perspective views and scenes illustrating fallen majesty and a sense of *sic transit*, where groups of local peasantry were pictured sprawled on broken columns, or cooking among the

ruins of imperial greatness. There was immense appeal to eighteenth-century sensibility in the idea of the contrast between the grandeur of the past and the descent into the squalor of the present; in the thought of the throne room of an emperor's palace inhabited now by a family of Slav fisherfolk.

The evidence suggests that Adam's principal concern in publishing his book was the enhancement of his reputation by appearing as the author of a splendid folio. In this almost shameless campaign of self-promotion, he was less concerned with questions of strict archaeological accuracy; and Clérisseau, perhaps because he found he was to be given so little of the credit for his contribution to the volume, was even less particular about this matter.

Fig. 29. General plan of Spalato, with the Palace forming the right-hand section of the modern town, the whole enclosed by the Venetian fortifications.

Plates which aimed to convey a romantic view of antiquity might be made more exotic still by the introduction of the *capriccio* technique, whereby, as in scene-shifting in the theatre, the buildings and monuments were moved about and adjusted to make a more evocative and atmospheric composition. A description in Consul Joseph Smith's catalogue of his collection of Canaletto pictures conveniently defines the *capriccio* style of representing townscape or topography as works being 'elegantly Historiz'd with Figures & Adjacencys to the Painters Fancy'.

There were, of course, varying degrees of imaginative manipulation of the facts in such *vedute*. In its most extreme form, a *capriccio* might be a wholly-imagined composition with actual buildings taken (as Count Algarotti said) 'from here or there' to form a truly whimsical grouping. In other cases, such as some of the plates of *Spalatro*, the element of caprice was slighter, with merely a feature or detail moved for effect. To such compositions appropriate human figures, characteristic of the locality, and typical vegetation might be added at will. In the *Spalatro* plates these figures were sometimes added by artists other than the draughtsman of the original compositions.

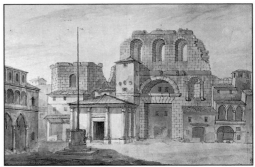

Fig. 30.   C.-L. Clérisseau: original drawing of the Porta Ferrea or west gate of the Palace.

Fig. 31.   F. Bartolozzi after C.-L. Clérisseau: annotated proof of the Porta Ferrea view.

The picturesque effect, and the romantic view of the past thereby conveyed – a topographical setting which mingled reality and fantasy – was more important than the scrupulously accurate representation of the site as it actually was.

Fig. 32.   C.-L. Clérisseau: original drawing of the interior of Diocletian's Mausoleum, converted into the Cathedral of Split.

Fig. 33.   D. Cunego after C.-L. Clérisseau: the Mausoleum, stripped back to its ancient appearance.

The *Spalatro* frontispiece includes a section of the Cryptoporticus, a sphinx from the Peristyle, a detail from a niche of the Porta Aurea, and a recumbent effigy taken from a Clérisseau drawing of the Temple of Augustus at Pola in Istria. The General Plan, itself a *trompe l'œil* marble tablet with illusionistic fixing-clamps, is surmounted by representations of the Temple and a section of the Mausoleum shown in ruins. A building in the perspective view of the Porta Ferrea loses a Gothic arcade, but the view gains a crowd of locals round a mountebank's stall. A view of the Mausoleum (now the Cathedral of Split) eventually published is quite different from the Clérisseau drawing in the Hermitage, St Petersburg. Modern people (including Clérisseau, shown at work) inhabit a building stripped of post-antique ecclesiastical fittings: they observe an interior such as they could not have seen in actuality. A perspective of the Temple has its background altered: buildings vanish, vegetation replaces them, and *staffage* appears. This, and another view of the Temple, are impossible, for in actuality it was entirely hemmed about by later building. Two groups of merchants in the published picturesque view of the Peristyle are not those shown in Clérisseau's original drawing in St Petersburg, but are lifted straight from a drawing of the Arch of the Sergii at Pola, to which Bartolozzi had added the figure-groups which were those eventually selected to 'historicize' the published engraving.

Fig. 34.   C.-L. Clérisseau: original drawing of the Temple, with buildings in the background.

Fig. 35.   F. Bartolozzi after C.-L. Clérisseau: the Temple, surrounding buildings removed, vegetation and figures added (annotated proof engraving).

Fig. 36.   F. Bartolozzi after C.-L. Clérisseau: another view of the Temple.

Fig. 37.   C.-L. Clérisseau: original drawing of the Peristyle, with portico to the Vestibulum at the far end, the Mausoleum through the arcade at left.

Fig. 38.   C.-L. Clérisseau (architecture) and
F. Bartolozzi (figures): Arch of the Sergii at Pola in Istria.

Fig. 39.   P. Santini after C.-L. Clérisseau: the Peristyle,
Bartolozzi's figures inhabiting Clérisseau's setting.

Other plates which purported to be accurate restorations of the ruins, aiming to show what the site had been like in late Antiquity, were themselves products of another kind of romantic imagination, but one which sought to convey an air of authority and verisimilitude.

Though these were not overtly picturesque, like the perspectives with their *capriccio* elements, nor designed to stir the sensibilities by the suggestion of decay and the passing of time, they were nevertheless based on a good deal of imagination beyond what the facts (as revealed by excavation and archaeological record, as well as deductions from reason, and by analogy and extrapolation) might warrant.

But what was the truth at which Adam aimed? In the plates he sought to provide a restoration of the palace as he thought it had been in Diocletian's time; and as this involved the exercise of Adam's imagination, it is clear that Fancy played a part in the search for Truth.

Adam would 'improve' upon the Romans by representing some architectural features – such as a pilaster capital of unusual form which he found in the Peristyle – not as they actually *were*, but as he

Fig. 40.   P. Santini after C.-L. Clérisseau: perspective view of the Cryptoporticus and marine wall of the Palace.

felt they *ought* to be. His own conceptions of taste and architectural propriety interfered with his role as an archaeologist recording the remains with scholarly impartiality. The 'improved' version of the evidence was something that could be adopted and applied with greater 'taste' in Adam's own architectural vocabulary. The pilaster capital was engraved in his book without any suggestion that this was Adam's interpretation of the evidence, regularized and beautified and ready to be used as a source or a model by himself in his 'Spalatro Order', subsequently a mainstay of his repertoire.

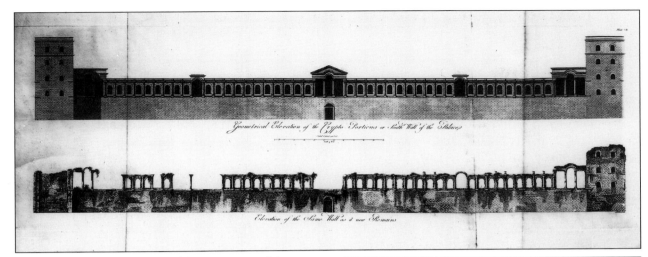

Geometrical Elevation of the Crypto Porticus or South Wall of the Palace

Elevation of the Same Wall as it now Remains

Fig. 41. A. Walker after R. Adam: treatment of the surviving Roman masonry of the Cryptoporticus and marine wall, with restoration.

Particularly interesting is the way in which Adam, perhaps inspired by Piranesi, restored the appearance of the Palace walls and gates in a series of plates distinguished both for their picturesque presentation and their technique of imaginative reconstruction. In these, views of the remaining ancient fortifications in their existing state are juxtaposed with geometric elevations of the same walls as they might have been. But it is not as simple as this; for the walls as shown are viewed as if through a 'time filter'. Adam stripped the surviving Roman masonry of medieval and later accretions (almost as a palaeontologist will dissolve with acid the matrix surrounding a fossil), and then he reconstructed what he imagined the original to have been.

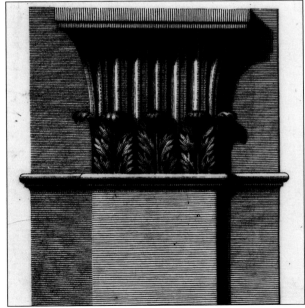

Fig. 42. Pilaster capital in the Peristyle of the Palace.

TASTE & ACCURACY; OR, GETTING IT RIGHT

The author of an archaeological and architectural volume always had to consider a number of vital matters potentially affecting the success of his undertaking, the business of 'getting it right'. These included: the general one of elegance of appearance – particularly important given the 'public relations' aspects of a book like Robert Adam's; authority of text, and correctness and credibility of plates; clarity of presentation; and the practical one of the economics of the publication.

Such books were extremely expensive ventures. Good advance advertising by prospectuses and in the periodical press was vital; a healthy and fashionable subscription-list, boosted by assiduous lobbying for the right names, was both useful in attracting further subscriptions, and in cushioning the author against financial loss.

It had to be borne in mind that a book would be read on different levels, and a one-volume work had to satisfy different sections of the market. A fellow architect would seize upon the measured drawings, for he might have bought the book for the use he could make of the plates in his own practice by adding new hints to his existing repertory of designs.

The rich and noble patron, idly turning the leaves of a finely-bound copy in his library, would be much more impressed by the *capricci*, the general views and attempts at reconstruction. He might have at the back of his mind the possibility of getting the clever author, or a rival architect, to design for him some elegant garden building, perhaps, based on a plate in the new book; and, if the result were successful, of commissioning a new front for his country seat, or an *à la mode* drawing-room ceiling in his London house. Such archaeological books were leaders of taste and fashion.

Getting it right meant ...

... ensuring that the PLATES were as accurate as possible and, above all, that they told the same story: that the perspectives were reconciled with the measured elevations, and that any apparent contradictions were eliminated. Although some plates were indeed altered, discrepancies between others remained unresolved, whether because Adam was then unable to check facts or to compare his drawings against the actual buildings, or because, quite simply, he did not notice errors or omissions, or even chose to disregard them.

The plates themselves were elegant: a reviewer praised the 'engraving part' of *Spalatro*, 'done by foreigners, with a taste and execution that never has been equalled in this country'. But the dichotomy between Truth and Fancy – between fact and fiction, Accuracy and Taste – was never completely reconciled. Adam, long back in London, looked over proofs of plates made in Venice from drawings by Clérisseau which in all probability Adam had never seen in their finished form; and he found that what Clérisseau had recorded did not match his recollections of what he himself had seen some years before, or accord with the detailed plans, sections and elevations the draughtsmen had prepared. The fact that many hands had been responsible for the whole

Fig. 43. C.-L. Clérisseau: original drawing of Porta Aurea with statues in niches.

Fig. 44. P. Santini after C.-L. Clérisseau: proof plate with annotation by Robert Adam.

Fig. 45. The Porta Aurea view corrected by removal of statues.

corpus of drawings, together with the time-lapse between actual survey and the checking of the engraved plates, meant that certain features were inaccurately published, or were even omitted altogether. There were some omissions and mistakes that no one involved with the project spotted, or did so only when too late. Adam seems to have concentrated on the large plans, and to have left Clérisseau to deal with some of the more picturesque buildings such as the Mausoleum, where the Frenchman's invention had been allowed full play. The unfortunate result, in this case, was that Clérisseau was found to have recorded as extant columns which Adam had shown correctly as missing.

Examples of Adam's problems in reconciling perspectives with measured elevations are the plates of the east wall. Here there was an anomaly between the representation of the round-headed windows as shown in the proof of the view published as Plate III, and in the geometrical elevation and restoration published as Plate X. This Adam noticed, and the perspective copperplate was reworked accordingly. In the case of the disappearing statues in the arcade of the Porta Aurea, Adam marked the proof with the comment that these sculptures 'were not remaining in the niches when I was at Spalatro, but I was inform'd they had been very lately remov'd'. The Venetian engraver Santini accordingly erased these products of Clérisseau's imagination.

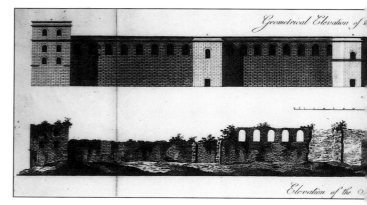

Fig. 46. *F. Bartolozzi after C.-L. Clérisseau: proof of view of Spalato from the east, showing Palace wall with inaccurately represented gate and windows of the patrol walk.*

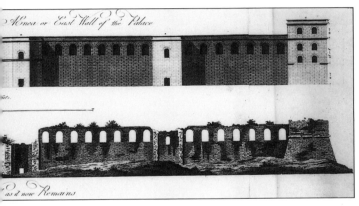

Fig. 47. *P. Mazell after R. Adam: geometrical elevation of extant Roman masonry of east wall, with restoration.*

Fig. 48. *Published state of Clérisseau's view corrected to correspond with Adam's measured elevation.*

... achieving a clear and accurate *TEXT* in the form of an Introduction and a commentary on the plates. Adam wrote this commentary in the form of a Description of the General Plan of the Palace, as he had restored it, together with an Explanation of the plates. His brother helped greatly in this task.

Study of the annotated proof plates makes it clear that Clérisseau was asked, through the agency of James Adam in Venice, to supply information required by Robert either to substantiate what he thought was the case, or else to remind him of particulars he had overlooked in what had been a fairly hasty survey of a very large building complex. The work of record and excavation had been hindered by the Venetian authorities' suspicion that Adam was in fact a spy, surveying the modern defences of the town and harbour. Although Adam prided himself on what he had achieved at Spalato in a short time – 'by unwearied application during five weeks, we compleated, with an accuracy that afforded me great satisfaction, those parts of our work which it was necessary to execute on the spot' – the expedition had clearly been rushed. Adam came away 'with all [his] operations in [his] pocket' after having spent, certainly, more time than Wood's nine days at Palmyra, but far less than the three months of Le Roy in Athens, the sixteen months of Desgodetz in Rome, and the two and a half years spent by Stuart and Revett in Greece.

Fig. 49.   F. Patton after R. Adam, the statues added by P. Sandby: proof with marginalia recording the opinions of C.-L. Clérisseau on the fabric of the building.

It is evident that the *Spalatro* team had been responsible for different aspects of the work of survey and record, and that Adam, as 'director', had not been able to look closely at everything. Nevertheless, it would be too cynical to put the most unfavourable interpretation possible on Robert's remark to James, in a letter written from Dalmatia, to the effect that he had been 'employed in considering the Antiquitys of this place', as implying that he had sat in the shade, with a cold carafe of wine, thinking great thoughts, while Clérisseau and the 'Myrmidons' worked in the August heat on *his* book.

Getting it right meant ...

... achieving maximum clarity of *PRESENTATION*. This was done, for instance, by introducing, as part of the letterpress of the volume, keys to plans of the Palace, rather than by crowding the plates with engraved 'labels' explaining the nature of individual rooms or suites of rooms.

Getting it right meant ...

... catering for the needs of *PROFESSIONALS*. The plates, especially the measured drawings of the orders and the enrichments, had to be furnished with accurate measurements which would satisfy architects who might use the book. Unlike Wood, or Stuart and Revett, who were not concerned that their books should be useful to architects as source books of decorative detail or stylistic motifs, Adam was probably much more anxious to see his book influence taste – and have himself recognised as the agent of that influence – as an aspect of his underlying self-advertising and 'image-making' aim.

Scholars and men of letters also would make use in their own historical work of a new publication deemed to be authoritative. In the year Adam's book came out, Edward Gibbon, on first contemplating the ruins of Rome, conceived the theme of his great history. He would later use Adam's folio, and was not wholly complimentary about its reliability: 'But there is room to suspect that the elegance of his designs and engraving has somewhat flattered the objects which it was their purpose to represent'.

Getting it right meant ...

... including a series of *JUDGMENTS* on the quality of the Palace as an example of late-antique architecture. The Explanation of the plates was advertised as containing 'Occasional Remarks on the Style of the Architecture'. These prove to be subjective comments and criticisms, designed to say as much about Adam's own architectural taste, judgment and abilities, as about those of Diocletian's architects and masons. This tendency was in direct contrast to Wood's policy as declared in the Preface to his *Palmyra*, to be but an impartial recorder leaving 'all criticism on the beauties and faults of the Architecture ... to the Readers'. Adam's discreet criticisms of certain late-Roman architectural solecisms carried the implication that Robert Adam, Esquire, Fellow of the Royal Society and of the Society of Antiquaries of London, would *never* do such a thing in the house he was building for *you*.

Archaeological treatise and architectural manifesto *Spalatro* certainly was; but it was also much more than that.

The book was part of what we should now call Adam's 'marketing strategy': a public-relations exercise designed to impress potential clients by his scholarship, taste, and ability to apply the lessons of the past – and the knowledge of ancient private architecture derived from a pioneering exploration of a palace complex – to the designs of the present. Surely a man who knew so well the domestic arrangements of a Roman emperor could plan better than any rival a country house for a British earl! *Spalatro* was self-advertisement of a very grand kind.

From his early days in Rome, Adam had spoken of his desire to publish some great work which would help launch or further his career in Britain. In the Palace at Spalato he saw a chance, and took it: a contemporary appreciated clearly his intention, and noted that 'Mr Adams, Architect, gone to Spolatra wt. Assistants in serch of Antiquities for Publication'. While Adam posed as the discerning antiquary he also had, as a hard-headed business-man, an eye to the future. A book on a Roman palace was something new, as opposed to a work on

baths or temples which, though this might be founded on scrupulous research, appeared however to have less originality. In Spalato he had chosen 'a most propper subject for gaining applause & character in England'. The long drawn-out production process may even have been advantageous, for the book thus appeared when Adam was already established, and when the public-relations effect of the subscription-list could do him most good.

Adam's ambition is manifest in this subscription-list, which is as much a statement of social success as it is proof of the author's architectural reputation and his standing as a scholar. Patrons or would-be connoisseurs wished to be associated with such a work, as the very act of subscription might be seen as a demonstration of their awareness of movements in fashion, tides in taste, or trends in design, as archeological exploration made available sources of inspiration for architectural and decorative styles based upon the antique.

The original plan to dedicate the book to the Adam family's old patron the Duke of Argyll was dropped as 'too nationall' – too Scottish for the London-based and European-educated Robert. The intention then (something a 'little more showy') was to dedicate it to George II. The old king died while the book was still in production; but this bolder scheme was adhered to with the purpose of flattering the young George III, perhaps in the hope that, by comparing his taste and patronage with that of Diocletian, a commission to design a new royal palace might be forthcoming. (Clerk of Eldin recorded that it was a design of Robert's for a British royal palace that had attracted particular attention on his first setting up in London.) The Adam brothers' correspondence discusses ways to enhance the quality of the subscription-list, and so to 'puff' the book further. They thought of presenting a copy to Frederick the Great, in order to be able to put his name on the list. 'Prussia's the thing. Besides I know he loves books of this here nature greatly, so that it will rather oblige him to give him an opportunity of showing his taste. The éclat of his name would sell 100 coppys in the City'. Robert Adam, soon to be architect to the Hanoverian King of Great Britain, even toyed with the idea of enlisting the names of Cardinal York and the Pope.

Spalatro was in every way a sumptuous creation. The splendour of its physical form, especially of those copies in the magnificent scarlet bindings made for presentation to royalty, and also those for special patrons and clients (blue leather for Knights of the Garter, green for Knights of the Thistle, brown and without the *dentelle* for the less distinguished rich) was designed to reflect the grandeur not just of ancient Rome but of the vision of antiquity that was the heart of Adam's architectural creed.

Publication was delayed until the clamour over the appearance of Stuart and Revett's *Antiquities of Athens* had died down. Adam's presentation bindings then challenged those of Stuart. The dedication to King George III praised his architectural knowledge and taste – attributes the King in fact owed to Adam's rival William Chambers. In 1769, on the foundation of the of the Royal Academy of Arts, Adam presented to Chambers for the use of the Academy a scarlet copy of his book, doubtless in the hope of being elected to its membership. Chambers, as Treasurer, kept him out.

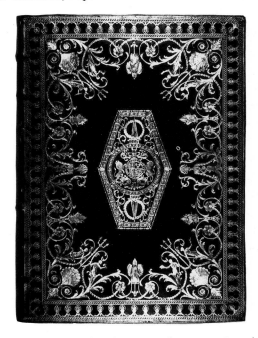

Fig. 50.   Copy of Spalatro *in red morocco Royal presentation binding.*

1754-1764: THE MAKING OF ROBERT ADAM

In 1754, the young Robert Adam was on the threshold of a European education. This was to turn a career which might simply have had Scotland for its field, and the design and construction of houses and public buildings for a local clientele as its staple aim, into a life of dazzling achievement and of international significance. The Italian experience, and its Dalmatian extension, had witnessed Adam's social, intellectual and artistic metamorphosis.

Ten years later, when *Spalatro* appeared, Adam was already established at the head of his profession. He had brought his 'Myrmidons' to Britain and, with draughtsmen from Scotland, he had established a drawing-office to handle the business which came to him rapidly. Soon he came to command what Mrs Montagu called 'a regiment of artificers', and could keep his clients waiting an hour. From his first establishing himself in London, he had attempted to show himself off to the very best advantage: this was 'the first flash of character', the initial stroke in the master-plan of advancement Robert had worked out in Rome. He had set himself up in a fine house, where potential patrons might inspect his drawings and see the pictures, sculpture and antiquities and casts of architectural mouldings he had acquired in Italy. Adam played the connoisseur, and his gentlemanly refinement was on display. 'With his taste, his productions, and his manners', wrote John Clerk of Eldin, 'everyone went away enchanted.'

By 1764, he had completed for a number of influential patrons some major country houses; he had recast others; he had created splendid interiors for houses designed by less talented architects. As a designer of public buildings he had made his mark on the townscape of London: Edinburgh was later to see his finest work in this field. As an architect of superbly planned town houses he had already begun a most distinguished series. In 1764 was founded William Adam & Company, the Adam brothers' firm of developers, speculative builders and builders' merchants which rapidly grew to be the largest building empire of the century, with vast and complex undertakings. The previous year Robert had written of the extent, variety and geographical spread of his own architectural practice 'which I am with difficulty able to get managed with Honour to myself & Satisfaction to my Employers'. He was, jointly with his great rival and senior contemporary, William Chambers, Architect of the King's Works.

In 1754, on the eve of his departure for Italy, he had inspected Westminster Abbey as a tourist. By 1764 he was launched on the career that would lead to a grave there.

Adam's public commissions, and equally his domestic designs, are testimony to his intense study of both the monumental and the private buildings of Antiquity, of which the Palace at Spalato is an instructive example. Colen Campbell, pioneer of British neo-Palladianism, had sought to 'introduce the *Temple* Beauties in a private Building'. Adam the eclectic tried to combine with the monumental an interpretation of what he thought was the domestic architecture of the Romans; and a resulting house such as Kedleston or Harewood, Syon or Osterley was a blend of his notion of 'the private edifice of the Ancients' with the grandeur of the *thermae*, temples, villas and public monuments which he had studied in Italy.

The publication at an opportune moment of his study of Diocletian's Palace served to bring Robert Adam even more to the notice of the polite world, to consolidate the reputation by then attained, and to carry to new heights a career already brilliant.

Labor omnia vincit
Virg. 1. Georg

Fig. 51.   C.-L. Clérisseau: capriccio of the Peristyle and Temple in ruins.

FURTHER READING

The letters of Robert Adam written to his family from Italy are the foundation of this essay, as they must be for the study of any aspect of the earlier life and career of Robert Adam. These form part of the Clerk of Penicuik Muniments in the Scottish Record Office, and quotations are made by kind permission of Sir John Clerk of Penicuik, Bt.

Of fundamental importance is John Fleming's classic study *Robert Adam and his Circle in Edinburgh and Rome* (London, 1962). The making of Adam's book is well discussed in detail in the same author's article 'The Journey to Spalatro', *Architectural Review*, CXXIII (1958), 103-107. This should be supplemented by the excellent analysis in Eileen Harris (with Nicholas Savage), *British Architectural Books and Writers, 1556-1785* (Cambridge, 1990). Also relevant are I. G. Brown, 'Ruins & Reputation: Robert Adam at Spalato', *The Art Quarterly*, 10 (Summer 1992): and *idem*, 'Archaeology & Ambition: Robert Adam and Diocletian's Palace at Split', *Minerva*, 3, no. 4 (1992). On Adam's sources and the development of his style see Damie Stillman, *The Decorative Work of Robert Adam* (London, 1973). On Clérisseau there is now Thomas J. McCormick's *Charles-Louis Clérisseau and the Genesis of Neo-classicism* (Cambridge, Mass., 1990). On the Palace at Split see Ernst Hébrard & Jacques Zeiller, *Spalato: le Palais de Dioclétien* (Paris, 1912); Georg Niemann, *Der Palast Diokletians in Spalato* (Vienna, 1910): T. Marasović, *Diocletian's Palace* (Belgrade, 1982); and J. J. Wilkes, *Diocletian's Palace, Split* (Sheffield, 1986). The special bindings of Adam's book are discussed in a forthcoming article by I. G. Brown '"With an uncommon splendour...": the Bindings of Robert Adam's *Ruins at Spalatro*', *Apollo*, CXXXV (November 1992).

SOURCES OF THE ILLUSTRATIONS

Figures 23, 24, 25, 31, 35, 42, 44, 46 and 49 are taken from the NLS set of proof plates of *Spalatro*.

Figures 26, 27, 33, 36, 41, 47, and 48 are taken from other copies of *Spalatro* in the National Library of Scotland.

Figures 28, 29, 39 and 40 are taken from the unbound set of *Spalatro* plates in the collection of Sir John Clerk of Penicuik, Bt., and are reproduced by his kind permission.

Figures 30, 32, 34, 37 and 51 are reproduced by permission of the State Hermitage Museum, St Petersburg.

Fig. 1.   National Portrait Gallery.

Fig. 2.   Reproduced by permission of the Trustees of the British Museum.

Figs. 3-4. From *Livre nouveau, ou regles des cinque ordres d'architecture, par Jacques Barozzio de Vignole* (Paris, 1757). NLS.

Fig. 5.   From *The Works in Architecture of Robert & James Adam* (London, 1778). NLS.

Fig. 6.   From *Le Antichità Romane,* Vol. II. (Rome, 1756). NLS.

Fig. 7.   From *Vedute di Roma* (Rome, 1748). NLS.

Fig. 8.   Reproduced by courtesy of the Trustees of Sir John Soane's Museum (AV 56/59).

Fig. 9.   From *Il Campo Marzio dell' Antica Roma* (Rome, 1762). NLS.

Fig. 10.   Reproduced by permission of the Trustees of the British Museum.

Fig. 11.   From G. B. Piranesi, *Le Antichità Romane,* Vol. I. (Rome, 1756). NLS.

Fig. 12.   Reproduced by permission of the Trustees of the Victoria & Albert Museum, London.

Fig. 13.   Reproduced by courtesy of the Trustees of Sir John Soane's Museum (AV 28/1).

Fig. 14.   Reproduced by courtesy of the Trustees of Sir John Soane's Museum (AV 10/18).

Fig. 15.   Reproduced by courtesy of the Trustees of Sir John Soane's Museum (AV 55/8).

Fig. 16.   From *Les ruines des plus beaux monuments de la Grèce* (Paris, 1758). NLS.

Fig. 17.   From *Les édifices antiques de Rome* (Paris, 1682). NLS.

Fig. 18.   British Architectural Library Drawings Collection/Royal Institute of British Architects (L12/5/7).

Fig. 19.   From *Fabbriche Antiche disegnate de Andrea Palladio* (London, 1730). Glasgow University Library.

Fig. 20.   From *A Journey into Greece* (London, 1682). NLS.

Fig. 21.   From *Entwurff Einer Historischen Architectur* (Leipzig, 1725). NLS.

Fig. 22.   From E. Hébrard & J. Zeiller, *Spalato: le Palais de Dioclétien* (Paris, 1912), as reproduced in *The Birth of Western Civilisation*, ed. M. Grant. Thames & Hudson (London, 1964 & 1986).

Fig. 38.   Reproduced by permission of the Syndics of the Fitzwilliam Museum, Cambridge (3618).

Fig. 43.   British Architectural Library Drawings Collection/Royal Institute of British Architects (B4/1).

Fig. 50.   Reproduced by permission of the British Library Board.

Decorations on pages 8, 14 and 48 are taken from *Livre nouveau ... par Vignole*. NLS.

The tail-piece on page 49 is taken from G. B. Piranesi, *Lapides Capitolini* Rome 1762. NLS.

Printed in Scotland for HMSO   Dd 8176930 C10 5/92 (36994)